MW01615376

My Ancestors Told Me ...

Writing from the Students at
Brooklyn East Collegiate Middle School

NY WRITERS COALITION PRESS
SPRING 2018

ISBN: 978-1-7323640-0-4
Library of Congress Control Number: 2018946855

Editors: Shanté Cozier & Carla Jeanpierre
Layout and Design: Nicole Di Luccio
Cover: Nicole Di Luccio

My Ancestors Told Me ... contains writing by members of
NY Writers Coalition's workshop at Brooklyn East
Collegiate Middle School

NY Writers Coalition Press, Inc.
80 Hanson Place, Suite 604
Brooklyn, NY 11217
(718) 398-2883
info@nywriterscoalition.org
www.nywriterscoalition.org

Contributors :::::

Amelia DeVerteuil

Edwige Edouard

Rasheed Johnson

Iziah Langdon

Daniel Mitchell

Gabrielle Polonio

Romario Roberts

Arianna Smith

Contents :::::

:: *Foreword* ::

One would think that after three sessions of writing workshops with the same kids, the facilitators would be burnt out. But for us, the answer is absolutely not! In fact, this session has been one of our favorites! Our young writers have matured in ways that we could not imagine. They are talented and wise despite being 12, 13 and 14.

Faithfully, every Friday, we started each session by sharing feelings about the day or our week, and each writer responded in ways that always surprised us: "I am feeling excited to try a new sport this weekend," or "I am feeling bad about a test score because I know I could have done better." Their self-awareness is more than noteworthy. We felt as though we were talking to our own friends. This workshop reminded us that just because our writers are children, that doesn't mean they are incredibly different from us. They are perceptive and imaginative and well-aware of the perils of this world.

The title "My Ancestors Told Me..." came from a poem written by one of our writers. It is also inspired by what we as facilitators witnessed soon after giving them a suggested writing prompt. As in our previous books, each piece in this collection has been written freely. That is, the participants used our suggested prompt to write whatever came to mind in that moment. It is as if their small hands were guided by the giant minds of our ancestral spirits, enhancing and enlivening their ideas with the same wisdom and fortitude used to navigate their everyday lives. Their pieces are all fiction, but the realness of their words gave us chills because we know they have captured reality and heart-breaking moments of truth.

What at times is painfully evident is that our young writers hear everything that is happening around them. They demonstrate a keen sense of who they are in spite of having many more years to live. In their writing is felt a sense of danger and an understanding of the unpredictability of life even when love abounds. There is greed and selfishness and chaos and violence. There is racism and there are guns, but there is also the enduring legacy of humanity to beat the odds and survive what seems insurmountable.

In our workshops, learning is tangible in the real sense of the word. We learned from them—everything from their code for needing to use the bathroom, to knowing when they were giving another student shine, or when they liked or agreed with an idea. This kind of learning and trading of language leaked into their writing. And they created worlds on the page!

It is with great joy and pride that we present this book to you!

Carla & Shanté
Facilitators at BEAST 2018

who Am I

Amelia
Age 12

WHO I AM

Amelia
Age 12

My Mother's Womb

I am now on the outside
unprotected by a barrier
and I move with my own two feet.
I speak amongst my thoughts
And the goals I make I'll seek.
But sometimes I wish to
Feel what I feel and be
Proud in my own personal
Room and those are the
Times I think back to my
Mother's womb.

I Am 7 Years Old and It's My Birthday

I woke up one morning
And looked at my feet.
Wow I already had a growth spurt
Man, that's neat!
I opened my door and closed
My eyes to try to pretend I
Was surprised. My mom and
My dad had waited for me
While I was asleep
They saw my face and
Shouted to me
Wow, you're 7! It's a very special week.
Wow, I'm 7! Almost a preteen.
Hooray!

Daniel
Age 13

My Mother's Womb

The warmth, the passion, and the love that I was given. I love her & she loves me. That's why she cares so much for me, even though I am just a parasite leeching off the ways she's cared for me. I take most of her nutrients, and when the time is right I leave her feeling empty inside. I love you mom, and thanks for caring, but I need all of this life and I'm not planning on sharing.

Amelia
Age 12

The Face of my Father

I share the face of my father, a man who refused to stop working hard all for his family. I share that motivation, working harder and harder and as the days pass, I see my shape develop and change, my perfect black skin getting darker. I won't stop until I rise up, until my family wises up, gets smarter, and understands the world better. I'll keep my eyes open and look at the world with a better view.

Older Now

I am 7 years old, and it's my birthday. When I was six, no one took me seriously. I was a child inexperienced. Baby, immature. Just another little devil here to break everything, screaming, crying, and laughing, bringing chaos wherever I went. But now I'm seven, a grown child, a baby adult. I'm older, and as they say, "The older, the wiser." Like cheese, the older it is, the better it tastes. I'm seven years old, and it's my birthday. I'm older now.

Arianna
Age 14

Love

I love you baby girl
Come here you mama's boy
Both are loved the same

Daniel
Age 13

Edwige
Age 12

Factory

I think back to my mother's womb, realizing how birth works like a factory.

    Step 1: Creation – when you're inside the womb

    Step 2: Process – growing slow and steady wins the race

    Step 3: Reinforcing – make sure it stays safe by not doing the wrong things

    Step 4: Packaging – It's almost ready; in a few short weeks, it will be on the way

    Step 5: Shipping and Handling – Just a few more days and we'll be here

    Step 6: We're here! = "Push! Push!" and we're almost here

    Step 7: Enjoy! We have arrived.

Who Am I?

I'm not underground on even on the ground. I'm not a flight contraption, but I DO fly. I'm not big nor small, not strong nor weak. I have claws, not paws, and I am giving my babies some tasty worms. I scout for some berries, nuts, and small animals. I'm like a crow, but not. However, I am a "superhero." Who am I? Oh, and one more hint: I'm a famous football's home team. Who am I?

Jimmy The Square

"Come on Jimmy! Be there or be SQUARE!" Those were the last words I ever heard before turning into a two dimensional waste of space. The only thing I can do is absolutely nothing. I want to walk upstairs, but I fall down. I want to eat, but I have to be face down. I want to play, but I can't because I have no hands. I'm just a stupid 2-D block. Why does this only happen to me? But hey, at least I'm not like Nonagon Billy, 9 painful sides to bore, walking onto everything and just being a huge blockade. But he gets to have legs and arms. Unlike me, a parallelogram of only 7 equal sides and no hope of being happy.

For the Past 7 Years

The past 7 years has been upsetting
The past 7 years has been uplifting
The past 7 years was an emotional rollercoaster

For the past 7 years ....

I am 7 seven years-old and it is my birthday. The past 7 years has been a fun ride—a good time. A good night in any way I can perform. Innovation is what is presented on the table. Creation was the new cake on the table, preventing their lives from deteriorating. And me, the blockade to preventing the delay of trade. For the past 7 years, I've been a good person.

For the past 7 years ....

Gabrielle
Age 12

As I Lay

As I lay in my bed, and think "What is the oldest memory I have?" I try to think back to my mother's womb, but I end up on my face in a playground at 3pm. Then I think further back to when 1 was on my face, at 2. Gosh, no wonder I look like this. After many memories of me falling on my face, I fall asleep. I dream that I'm floating around in a pool of some fluid and a stupid chain is attached to my belly button. I kick and yell, and then something rubs against my body from the outside. I wake up immediately after, and I don't remember anything.

My Grandmother's So Disappointed

My Grandmother's So Disappointed
All she wanted is for me to be anointed
I'm a girl from off the streets, what you expecting
You think I'm gonna walk up in here, always respecting
This is my mouth, I could say what I like,
And just because I'm here that don't mean it's always right!
It's not my fault they crossed the line
That's their problem, not mine.

Black Girl Magic

Black Girl Magic
Black Girl Pride
Black Girl Greatness
That's Black Girl Identified

Black Girl Feel
Black Girl Melanin
Black Girl Love
That's Black Girl Evidence

Forgotten

Have you forgotten me?
The person who took care of you for so many years?
The person who you depended on all your childhood?
The person you suddenly turned your back on?
Have you forgotten me?

Iziah
Age 12

Green

I am green, greener than the Grinch. But I don't lie. Just because I'm green, doesn't mean I'm mean.

Rasheed
Age 12

Rasheed
Age 12

Memories

Memories of my mind
I try to find
I see it far
I see it near
I may just be a speeding deer
My memories wander
That is true
Like when I fell off my bike
in the zoo
My memories of my heart break was mangled
As I watch it tore limb
By limb
Or cover
By cover
As I watch time pass by

Mother's Womb

I think back to my mother's womb
When I was reborn,
I think back to the time when I first had a fight
I think back until everything was erased
I think back but I stopped to notice it was too late
I think back to 7th grade when I used to run up and
down the block to holler at girls instead of going to
    learn
Now I stop again to look at myself and think what
    have I done
And back to the life I had thought I'd won

25

Romario
Age 12

Who Am I?

Who Am I?

Am I aligned

With a certain

Class

Or

Am I

The one above all

Son of Saul

Or

Am I

The one who

Led the fall

Arianna
Age 14

Forgotten

Have you forgotten me mama? I thought I was your baby. Remember you used to cuddle me, laugh with me and call me pumpkin pie. You and daddy loved me, but one day you went away. But then you came back. Then you went away some more. After that you never came back. I was really sad. But then daddy started to cuddle me, laugh with me and call me pumpkin pie. He was the only one to love me now. I just hope he doesn't go away too.

Daniel
Age 12

LIGHT AND TRUTH

Amelia
Age 12

Your Life Is Short

Your life is short but I keep it from you,
why would I tell you something that makes you feel
    blue?
I have tried and tried to make you feel strong
but you've pushed it away and only like my songs.
The songs I sing to lift you up and float your boat,
only because it's your only ounce of hope.
But when I stop, you sulk and forget what I told you ...
I don't know how long I'll be with you.
I try to keep you away from the pain ...
and make it disappear ...
but it seems I'm the only one who cares.
I have shortened my life because of you ...
and I know that you can't repay the dues.
So for now on I'll sing a song for you
to empower you with hope
and relieve you of your blues.

Stephanie

Friday night was a night of dreams for Stephanie and her team. They ran to the house, broke down the door and landed on the 2nd floor. "We just want to party; we don't want to hurt nobody" is the phrase Stephanie and her crew always say. She is too caught up behind her nails as long as rulers and hair as fried as bacon to realize what she is doing. Stephanie's dignity was short, and so was she. Her image was dirty, and everything about her needed to be cleaned.

Memories of Her Mother

The memories of her mother were marked in her head. Some of the memories moved on while others didn't. The majority of the memories sat there and were mangled, while more were made. Even though memories were reborn, those mangled in her head didn't live to see another day.

The Teacher's Pet

I sat down hesitantly, right beside the teacher's pet. Our teacher handed out a piece of paper and my heart fell to my feet. When the teacher's pet wrote, I wrote. When she stopped, I did too. It was like taking candy from a baby! When she finished her test, I stood right behind her, thinking about all of the praise that would come my way! Until the teacher's pet whispered something in her ear, and later on I was the only one in the classroom sitting in the same seat tapping my pencil against the desk, wishing none of this happened. Worst of all, I didn't even pass.

Mondays!

When I wake up in the morning, all I see is a blur. And my mom's face shaking me while my dog sits at the door.

When I go to the bathroom, all I see is yellow while the light shines on my face and tries to make me mellow.

All I see is black, which isn't a color but a reflection of my mood when my mother lays out my uniform to go to school.

All I see is light, but it is very far away and all I hope 4 is days to pass all the way to Friday.

Lunch

Snap, crackle, pop. You make my heart stop. Taste the rainbow. Your colors make me drop. I love that you smile back at me while I rip you open, and the way to describe you is simply unspoken. And my little ones who are gone in a bite make me soar to a wonderful flight. The artificial ones who leave me with a print cause me to be orange-handed, rather than red-handed, while I'm taking a drink. Hmmnnn ... What wonderful things I do for you.

I have Fallen Into Something

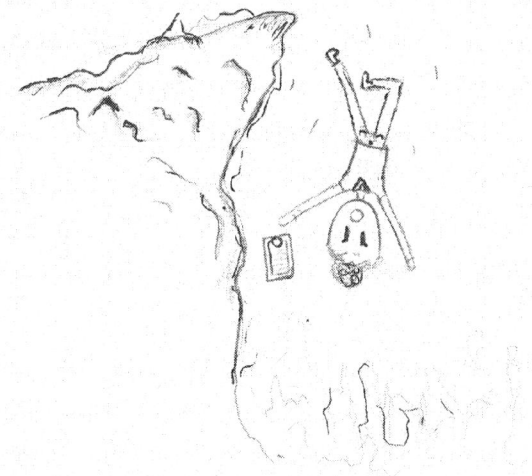

Amelia
Age 12

The Epitome of Greed

She never wanted what she had and always asked for more. She was never satisfied with a dollar because it wasn't enough. She always threw fits and lied to get her way, and she still does it to this very day. She was a brat and disregarded everybody and wanted to gain and gain. Her mind was fixated on the newest every-thing—newest shoes, newest clothes. She lacked gratefulness and was the epitome of greed.

Thief

You've always been jealous of me because I have something that is actually appealing. You prance around and always take things that aren't even yours and hold a scythe so I understand. Once you've flown upstairs into my room, you actually don't look quite as evil as you usually do. You've stolen this from me, but it's fine. Your actions were cruel, but it's not like I even care, I still have my integrity.

I Will Not Forget You

Have you forgotten me? I am your friend. We have gone through so much, but now you look at me as an outcast, and I am disappointed. Where have we gone? Look at us. We are so trapped in our own mindset that we can't determine right from wrong. We move with our feet, not with our hearts. What was once a fun and true moment with you is now an awkward, miserable time. You have forgotten me, but I will not forget you.

Daniel
Age 13

We Just Wanna Party

A party? What is it?
Is it used to celebrate?
Celebrate. What is there to celebrate?
Do we celebrate
The pain of wanting to change
to be widely accepted
and respected as a person in a full world?

This world is a place of pain and hope
where one move
Can ruin your faith in life.
Is life a game?
It is not a game.
This is pain and we must restrain
ourselves from drifting away.

Changes

Everything is just as it was when I left. I can still hear
the birds. I can still smell the freshly baked bread from
the bakery a few blocks away. I can taste the orange
in my mouth, and I can still feel the floor as I walk to-
wards my house. I can hear the cars pass by. Nothing
has changed except me.

Edwige
Age 12

A Healthy Statue

Life is short but there is only one thing I'm focused on.
Love is the thing I want.
Love is basically a trap worth falling into.
Love never leaves.
Success is another thing I focus on.
Success almost spells see: to see another conflict.
Success and love is a reaction to the product of
    happiness
However you need to dig.
Dig deeper—dig, dig for the treasure you want.
This is America.
You gotta wait for the man wearing black on a white
    horse.
You gotta wait till he is possessed.
Then you have to escape.
The statue that is waiting starts chipping.
Chipping away your healthy bones.
Each chip tells a story.
Each chip possesses a year.
Make your statue healthy.
Each block shows ...
Something.
Make smoother statues that are also like you.
Take all the hits.

Edwige
Age 12

Rainbow

Monday is for maroon, as in depression.
Tuesday is for teal, as in lightheadedness.
Wednesday is for water, as in blue and clear.
Thursday is for turquoise, as in joyful.
Friday is for fun, as in there is no color that
    could be wrong.
Saturday is to be joyful and to explore the
    world;
Everyone is even, no matter what color.
The stereotypes are meant for hurting, not for
    suggesting.
The rainbow comes when the package of roses
    are red
and violets are blue,
And so on.

Gabrielle
Age 12

We Just Want to Party, We Don't Want to Hurt Nobody

We left before 7
Decided to seize the night
We were the first ones there
Now no one could pick a fight
The museum started pumpin'
And so did our fists
The drinks were passing round
You get the gist
Everyone had a good night
No one kept track of time
Everyone stayed on the dance floor
Even Nicolette Narime

Days

I associate Monday with Grey. A bad + stormy day.

Tuesday is Yellow. It could be good, but may be just a bit much.

Wednesday is Blue. It is the middle of the week. A checkpoint.

Thursday is Black. Extremely boring as you wait for the next day.

Friday is Beige. It is nice, bright day, and marks the weekend.

Saturday is Gold. Pretty self-explanatory.

Sunday is brown. School is the next day.

And the cycle starts again.

Iziah
Age 12

Sorry, Not Sorry

Me
Sin
Not
Atoned
God
Angry
But
Not
Sorry

Have Your Forgotten Me?

Have you forgotten me?
I turn around and see an old box
"Have you forgotten me?" it said again.
"It must be an old toy with some battery left."
I looked through the box and found a childhood
memory, my stuffed animal that can speak. I used to
have it in the morning and in the night, even in the
bathroom. Until my dad took it away from me I had
    forgotten it.
"I missed you," I said and broke into tears. Me, a 33
year old man, crying from a stuffed animal. But I did-
n't care. I missed it for real.

Iziah
Age 12

Rasheed
Age 12

Romeo & Juliet

Romeo, oh Romeo
Oh how I love my Romeo
Juliet, Juliet I wish you would never leave my side
While the days pass by
I am going to the moon,
my love
And I will return soon
Keep this in mind
Life is like a ladder
it's full of ups and downs
So now you know
why don't you throw
Down that ladder
So I can give you my heart
You are my love, my one true love
And it hurts to say goodbye
When you are inside
My heart is full of lullabies
But don't worry my sweet
I'll be sure to bring back some cheese
I just wish your parents would open the door
Even if I beg on the floor
Now let's say our goodbyes
Cause the faster I go up
The faster I come back down

Their Eyes *Were* Watching God, Wow!

Their eyes were watching God, wow! That's strange because God normally watches us. The days when we grew up, but the sun sank down and how the world spins round and around. But the things you must remember is to cherish the moments because life goes up, and may come back down.

Acronym

Machines
Yourself
Hexagon
Apple
Teacher
Easter
Richie
Sucker
Kim
Elephant
Exchange
Party
Meter
Extra
Good
Olive
In
Need
Grow

These are the words that makes me love the day. This is what I get up for. This is what I love to hear. ANSWER: MY HATERS KEEP ME GOING.

Romario
Age 12

Love is What

What is love?
Is it passion
That gets weaved
Into a misled fashion

Is it this thing
That drives me to say I have
Come to take you
Back

The simple fact
That every
Second that
Flies by
Is worthless
In my eyes
Without you

My Mother's Womb

I think back to my mother's womb
Where I just learned
How to rhyme
The days where
Everything was perfect

I was a young boy
Just learning how to work it
But after a while
The world gave me
Her beautiful smile and
Said, "Boy, you gotta change that style."
She said, "It's prime time to learn how to live."

Mama I know I have to shine
All is mine
Never has love been a crime

"Have you tried being respectful and getting a Job?"

"What's "Respectful?" and I have to go... Thanks for nothing."

"Mmhmm..."

Edwige
Age 12

IN DANGER

Amelia
Age 12

The Radio Weapon

It was eight o'clock. I had just come back from night school. I ran over to my bed, took off my shoes, and layed in it. My roommate was out partying and left a note saying not to touch her radio. Why would I even want to? It was a weapon used to burst open my ear drums. I walked to the fridge to take out Vitamin Water, but when I touched the handle there was a vibration. Even though I took my hand off, it was still there. I knew what was coming—music—playing all night long. I stopped myself from punching a hole in the wall. Despite that, my anger was building up, so I grabbed the note on the radio, ripped it up, and threw the radio on the ground. Music in my dorm was never to be heard again.

Darkness

You wouldn't expect something so innocent to be so dark. It is slow beating and it feels like a dart. It is not bright. It is not lust, when you look inside of it, it is covered with dust. You want it to keep you alive and in full thrust, but instead it sits inside you like a big clump. For some people, it's a different story and gives no worry, but in this case it's ....

You Told Me This Was the Right Way

You told me it was the right way, but in fact it was wrong. I screamed, running down a hill until I fell into a pond. My shoes were muddy, my clothes soaked, and my hair the only thing dry. Then, I started to speed walk because I spotted an owl looking me straight in the eye. I went deep into a forest and saw a hive of bees, and I thought to myself, "Why me?!" While walking even deeper into the forest, I regained my confidence and looked death straight in the eye, staring above at the gloomy sky. This Monday was not my day, and it fell apart when I read a sign, "Go Straight!" NO WAY!

Car Accident

This is a luxury. It can be taken away. You control it until this very day. You wandered on the lonely street, yet when it came you pushed it to its peak. And when you lost your focus, you wouldn't think that your luxury would begin to sink. It was unexplainable and very embarrassing when you saw it bubble; you could barely bare it. Stop losing your focus and be responsible because the world already has its flow, but it's you who must push go.

Hunger

Jane walked down the New York Streets to grab a bite to eat. Whether it was a pizza or a BLT, Jane was hungry and her hunger couldn't be beat. She thought about pizza, she thought about more. She even went to Popeyes and stared at the door. But then Jane had a thought and began to run. Why not go to Chick-fil-A again? While running, Jane's steps get slower and slower. Jane stopped and had no clue that a big wad of blue bubble gum was at the bottom of her shoe. Jane was disgusted by what she had found and walked back home sulking with her head down.

Watch Me

I went against the odds.
Why? Because the one father I had
Who not only watched over me
But all of the world's people
Is no longer with me.
Even in the midst of the pain in the world as a whole,
Innocent people killed because of the afro on their
    heads
Or the beautiful, rich skin they wear and own
He is no longer watching me.
No longer answering my prayer
While I crouch on the floor with my hands to the sky.
I have done something terrible and even God is mad
    at me.

Am I Wrong?

Please let me know why I am wrong
Am I wrong for fighting for what's right,
While you put a gun to my chest?
I'm trying to speak up like my ancestors once told me,
So why is this wrong?
It's ironic —the things you do to me
And while you force me into the cop car
I say, please have mercy on me
.

The Aftermath

He used a gun to break our hearts
Our families, our lives are falling apart.
We search for some way to push us back to shore,
But instead we are tortured by another downpour
It punctured our hearts and messed with our souls,
But we should try to stand and be bold
Let's not let him get to us and make us feel as if he has
    won
Even as we look back at all the damage he has done

Arianna

Age 14

Fire Alarm

The fire alarm went off and we thought it was a fire drill. Then we heard gunshots. First, there was only one. Then two. The teachers shushed us. And we all listened in silence. Then 1, 2, 3, 4. They were coming from both sides of the school. Everyone in class went into a panic. Kids were screaming and crying. You could hear the same things in other classrooms. Teachers had fear in their eyes. I heard one girl scream out "Oh God, no!" But I just sat there with my hands against my ears and my eyes shut, having flashbacks of my whole life up until now.

Rasheed
Age 12

Daniel
Age 13

Purple

The color purple reminds me of the days and times I spent in Wakanda. Remember the times I've died trying to duplicate and replicate that dream. A dream—a way to manifest pictures into the brain and to get creative in different ways. Try to remember that dream as you're walking down Front Street. But stay focused for one reason only. If you have forgotten, remember now getting hit by Alaris was painful, so don't stop and think in the middle of the street because your life will end pretty quickly, if you do.

The Quiet American

The president owns. We are forced to love and care for him, but we are free as Americans. We will be what we need to be. I read these words one day and I thought, they're right. We should fight for our rights and speak our minds, but what can I do sitting here wondering what to do. I stay here lying to myself saying there is no chance for me to help represent or to speak for my country, to fight for us and live my life the right way, the correct way. I can't because I'm too shy. I better keep my mouth shut and be my own person.

Mad Gods

The gods are mad at me. They hurt me. They hate me. They've killed me and brought me back to torture me. I have joined their enemy to fight against them. They tortured me. Power I've never had before. They kill me again. I am like Luke Castellan. And they want to kill me.

POP! No Warning

With the first POP, it was fine. After the second, I got worried. Usually after the first POP, the principal would call from the loud-speaker warning whoever it was to stop, but this time there was no warning. This time a student didn't bring fireworks. He brought a gun. A school-wide panic began. As everyone fled out of their classrooms towards the front of the building, I stayed quiet running into a closet. That's why most people I know are now dead.

People shoot instead of talking it out. People want to kill instead of wanting to heal. That is why we need to stop it. Stop the violence. America, "Home of the Brave," we say. How can we be brave with the threat of death looming around?

Edwige
Age 12

Wings and Float

A dangerous man was out on the streets today. He killed a woman, and lock-picked her car. But he was only 14 and unable to drive, so he stole his mother's wallet. He went 60mph in a residential area. "Highlights made it quick, and he lived a high life on the weekends." He gave up his youth for this and he wanted it. This all happened and the news anchorman said, "Last night was a car crash. The sirens blared. He gets so caught up in his own head." His mother said, "When are you coming home?" He never came home. He started to fade, losing what he wants anymore. It feels just like the end of the world. Before this incident, his girlfriend said, "Sometimes things are just for the best. Better all the way."

A Good Scare

It was October 31st and the kids were all prepared for king-sized chocolate bars, 90 year-old candy that actually tastes decent, jaw breakers, and a special taffy. However, this wasn't the place to get candy. There was just prunes 5 years too old, cashews, and left over food. But there was still one special house NO ONE went to. The house was rooted to the ground that not even the most strongest tornado known to man can even move one inch. The house looks like a medieval-aged house with a telephone wire running through it. The things that happened in this house are too unbearable to blurt out. Six dead people are in the basement, a bone on the curved stairs, and a bed that looked like it was never unwrapped, yet had 40 year old mold on it, and a broken balcony. A clear mask is his cache—the mask of the unknown.

Those Are Just Fireworks

The day was March 3rd. My friends and I went to a concert in Georgia. We really enjoyed the artist's songs except for the 17th one. I'll never listen to that song again. "Those are just fireworks," a friend of mine said. But it was really someone shooting towards the concert at a long range. We didn't know why, but we ran. We ran to leave as people lay dying left and right. One person had said that they were fireworks but .... It was just a setup—one big setup.

What type of "America" is it when people don't listen? What type of "America" is it when people define guns as beautiful and God's gift?

This type of America.

Gabrielle
Age 12

Portals

These are like Portals
They give you the ultimate privacy
It may be easy to get in
But once you're in, you want to get out
This is where you recharge
Or just dispose of waste
This is where you disobey your mother
And this is where you cry
Each and every one brings a different mood
It's your choice to decide which one you go through

$$\frac{life}{3 \ years \ letts}$$

beautiful,

50% terible

gay

Iziah
Age 12

Iziah
Age 12

God's Plan

I was singing God's Plan in my head & then was greeted by a young man who wished to come in. I said, "Yes." He said God wanted us to make the US bigger, from coast to coast. It was called manifest destiny.

Gun Violence

The fire alarm went off, and we thought it was a fire drill. Then we heard gunshots. We were screaming and crying. The teacher quieted us down and we all hid in silence. Dead Silence. For hours we sat huddled together silently. If we all survive, I'll do all of my school work and pay attention in class. Another shot fired and I had a flashback of my whole life. I started crying.

Rasheed
Age 12

Self- Service

This notice is for those who think self-service is
the way.
But after they help themselves, don't feel
inclined to pay
I have done a lot of things in my life, here is what
I say
"Think first before you take more things with no
intent to pay"
Life is like a merry-go-round.
It makes you dizzy,
but just taking more stuff makes me feel drizzy.
I wouldn't be poor, that is true
I sell it one day that's what I do.
It's crazy to think you would never get caught
But when you're as smooth as me there is no
doubt.
I stole something I should have bought
But like many of my types
I was caught.

Have Mercy

I'm tired of going to school. I'm tired of learning too many things that we aren't even going to use till we are in high school. You know our little brains can only take little by little. We need time to grow. And not all at once, we just want to take it slow. I'm tired of hearing the same words: -1, -3, -5. I feel like my life is going up and down. This mystery is like a crisis waiting to be solved. But when you get in trouble, that's when you tumble down the hill. Then, the teacher calls my mom asking, "what did he do while he was in school?" I wonder if my mom is preparing for me to get home. I walk through the front door and yell out, "I'm sorry." I walk up the stairs and see my dad on the phone, and I hear my teacher to the tone. I go in my room to see my games and phone gone. I fall down and yell, "Have mercy on me!

Romario

Age 12

Reality's Dreams

I am 7 years old
And it's my birthday
The day that I was
Conjured into a form
I am no longer warm

Here comes the swarm
Called reality's embrace
I come face to face
With the world's worst nightmare

Reality
A fatality
When was it filled with
Proportionality
My God stands with me
Man bows to me

I am no longer 7 years old
My dreams have been told
Life set into mold
Life's meaning has been stolen

When shall I carry the
Burden of the guilty
I have no regards
For thy reality
Humans have no remorse
For the ones who pull the horse

So run within the shadows
Cradled
Confined in the
Devil's Marrow
Your hidden song
Is just too shallow

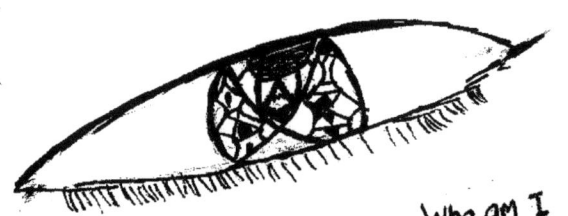

Who am I
Am I aligned
~~with~~ a certain
class
Or
am I
The one above all
Son of Saul
Or
am I
the one who
Led the fall

Romario
Age 12

WE WILL SURVIVE

Amelia
Age 12

My Pants Have Stitches and So Do I

When coming home from school on a rainy day, I ran straight past my house and went to the park. At the front of the street sign, I layed down my bag and played on the swings. The swings were so purple that I started to drift away while swinging. Then all of a sudden, I kicked too high and landed in the mud. I ran home. While standing at the front of my mother's house door waiting anxiously, I knocked, wishing I was in Wakanda.

My Plant

You were given to me with your stems all green and gave me a sense of excellency. I watered you everyday and stared at you from the window sill, while the clock ticked and outside started to chill- until I lost focus. You probably lost faith in me and I'm sorry about that. You were left on the heater, and I saw you misshapen with your petals all flat. And when I lifted you at the pot, your roots that helped you live were all black. So when you had started to bend, I took you near the sun because it isn't the end.

A Riddle

You're a bizarre one, but I love you. You help me through ob-
stacles, but I haven't seen you in zoos. You're a little short, but
I look up to you. You're from Africa and are a medium brown,
but I know you aren't from this town. You are my spirit and
start with an A and to this day, you are a huge part of my life.
Oh, what a wonderful, wild life!

Magic

Did you believe in magic? Because it doesn't look so. You
haven't changed our world. There is still criticism and by that,
I mean discrimination. They haven't changed at all. We can-
not repeat history, where white was said to be pure and black
was only ominous. When can it be equal? Why must they be
privileged, while we hope for change? Why is it about skin?
We must act sooner now. Do you believe in magic?

I have FALLE[N]
AnD DI[...]
but I didn't

Alex 55

Edwige
Age 12

to Something...
T MAKE IT!
NO! You can do it! JUMP!
He can't make it, He wanted to end it all along...
Peace & Love
Civilization 5 miles

Daniel
Age 13

Double Consciousness

In a time of death and defeat, I survived. If I hadn't done this, I would've died. I blame Hitler. He was looking for Jews. I am a Jew, but I have blonde hair and, as my neighbors told me, the bluest eye. I have heterochromia. It is very common, so one eye is blue and the other one is brown. The blue one is bright and shines like a diamond. The other one is dirty like a piece of charcoal. How did I decide to deal with it?

My Children

As I run away from life
I take my children with me
I hide them away because the world is dark and scary.
My children are great. Rare and innocent.
They are without a fear in the world.
I have no reason to change that.

As I run away from life, I take my children with me. I hide them away because the world is a dark and scary place. My children are great people and innocent without the world ruining them.

Edwige
Age 12

97

They say he's the 6-foot beast

They say that he is a legend.

They say he's the guard of this prison.

But not me.

About 3 months of planning and 7 months of crafting, I am ready to escape.

The name is 97, as in the 97th man trapped in here.

The bad service here made it a pain to withstand. However, I did it.

I jumped, I slashed, and even had to knock out a snitch. I grabbed a boat and started to drift off. I only had the bare minimum.

It wouldn't take long to notice 97 was out of his cell. They'd use anything to trace me. I'm off the radar but not for long. The cops are going to be aware and look out for me... until I go back and be tormented again. 97 to 98 and finally to 99. Only in.

A New Family

When he was a child, he prayed for a "restart" in life. He wished for another family—one that was 10,100, or even 1000 times better than his current one. He was 7 at that time. Every year he said in his mind, "I'll first pray, then blow out the candles. Therefore, I will have twice the luck!" He did as he said and blew out the candle. However, after basically 14 tries, God responded. After he went to sleep, he was scraped up by God's hands and drifted away—away to another family. Now that he's older, he prays for a "re-do".

Him and Her

They were in a 7-year relationship
Then they both predicted
when they would get rich a little bit

Then he said,
"We can do anything when we use our heads."

Black girl magic
Black boy joy
Nothing could penetrate the wall
They called it
The American Dream

They both agreed
To succeed
in getting the American Dream
Then he,
Filled with glee,
Said, "Please stay with me."

The girl agreed
And that's how they succeed
In the American Dream

Gabrielle
Age 12

When I Was Child

When I was child, I prayed that I would stay young forever. I never did want to be an adult, with all this responsibility. Ever since my father told me about taxes, I forgot about my dream of being grown and doing what I want. But now that I'm older, I pray that I stay this way forever. I've been paying taxes and rent for all my life. Being elderly is boring—sitting around all day, money being given to you like you can't provide for yourself. Responsibility isn't so bad after all.

Back in the Days

Back in the days we had to plug in the landline to the printer.

Now, we don't even need to be near it.

Amelia
Age 12

Rasheed
Age 12

God's Plan

When I was a child, I prayed for a miracle.
But now that I'm older, I pray for what every adult
    prays for—
A million dollars!
I remember when I was a kid that anything was
    possible,
but I had to learn the hard way as a grown-up that
    nothing can be possible when you have no ideas
    to fill the world with.
So now I have no choice but to give up and accept
    failure.
But then I thought to myself for a good while and said,
    no.
I will fulfill my dream.
I will stay strong.
I will be the little kid I used to be.
I will bring it out of me, I will win.
I will be God's plan.

Wishes

When I was younger
I wished for fun
None
Can surpass what I would
Die for
I shall apply force
This thing that I want
This thing that I need
Is pure
Never has it been filled with
Greed

Now that I'm older
I wish for love
Cry to the one that's up
Above
This thing called love
Fuels my existence
Duels the devil's impudence
Mewls over my to-do list

I am still new to this
So I wish and wish
Always served the
Same dish
So I call upon these things
That make me whole

The Brooklyn East Collegiate Middle School Writing Group

Acknowledgements :::::

We share the belief that the world is a better place when all voices can be heard.

Many thanks go to our foundation, government, and corporate supporters, without whom this writing community and publication would not exist: Allianz GI, Amazon Literary Partnership, Cowan Slavin Foundation, Emmanuel Baptist Church Benevolence Fund, Kalliopeia Foundation, Meringoff Family Foundation, The National Endowment for the Arts, The New York City Department of Cultural Affairs and the Two West Foundation. NYWC programming is also made possible by the New York State Council on the Arts with the support of Governor Andrew Cuomo and the New York State Legislature.

The Brooklyn East Collegiate Middle School Writing Club and this publication are made possible by the Art A Catalyst for Change Initiative, supported, in part, by public funds from the New York City Department of Cultural Affairs in partnership with the City Council and NYC Council Member Laurie Cumbo.

We rely heavily on the support of individual NYWC members and attendees of our annual Write-A-Thon and Red & Black Fundraiser. In addition, members of our Board of Directors have kept this vital, rewarding work going year after year: Timothy Ballenger, Tamiko Beyer, Louise Crawford, Atiba Edwards, Marian Fontana, Kaitlyn Greenidge, Ben Groom, Susan Karwoska, Brooke McCaffrey, Sophie McManus, Alexis Nixon, and NYWC Founder and Executive Director Aaron Zimmerman.

To find out more about NYWC and learn how you can sponsor a NYWC Press publication or program, please contact INFO@NYWRITERSCOALITION.ORG or call (718) 398-2883.

NY Writers Coalition

NY Writers Coalition Inc. (NYWC) is a 501(c)(3) non-profit organization that creates opportunities for formerly voiceless members of society to be heard through the art of writing.

One of the largest community-based writing organizations in the country, NYWC provides free, unique, and powerful creative writing workshops throughout New York City for people from groups that have been historically deprived of voice in our society, including at-risk and disconnected youth, homeless and formerly homeless persons, individuals who are or have been incarcerated, veterans of war, those living with disabilities, cancer, and other major illnesses, immigrants, seniors, and many others.

For more information about NYWC programs
and NY Writers Coalition Press publications visit
www.nywriterscoalition.org

Made in the USA
Columbia, SC
15 June 2018